S0-ANR-119

THE TRAVEL BUG

A TRAVEL JOURNAL FOR KIDS 7 TO 14

WRITTEN BY LINDA SCHWARTZ • ILLUSTRATED BY BEV ARMSTRONG

The Learning Works

Cover Design & Illustration
Beverly Armstrong
Text Design & Editorial Production
Sherri M. Butterfield
Composition & Graphic Production
Karen McCarter

*Gratefully dedicated
to Barbara Kern
for a super idea and
to Jeanette Honikman
and Kate Amerikaner
for their help.*

Copyright © 1993 by Linda Schwartz

All rights reserved. The purchase of this book entitles the individual classroom teacher to reproduce copies for use in the classroom. The reproduction of any part for an entire school or school system or for commercial use, by any means—electronic or mechanical, including photocopying and recording—or by any information storage and retrieval system, without the written permission of the publisher is strictly prohibited. Inquiries should be addressed to the Permissions Department,

The Learning Works, Inc.
P.O. Box 6187
Santa Barbara, California 93160

Library of Congress Catalog Number: 92-074104
ISBN 0-88160-256-6
LW 203

Printed in the United States of America. Current Printing (last digit): 10 9 8 7 6 5 4 3 2

Introduction

The Travel Bug has been created for you to enjoy while traveling. Its fun-filled pages provide a surefire way to ban backseat boredom and to cure those what-to-do blues. These pages offer dozens of ways to preserve both fleeting impressions and more tangible souvenirs. This book is divided into three sections: Preparations and Impressions, Puzzles and Games, and Journal Pages and Keepsakes.

PREPARATIONS AND IMPRESSIONS

Pages in the Preparations and Impressions section will help you prepare for your journey and give you opportunities to record your impressions of the trip. First, use the handy checklists to get ready. Next, make notes about the places you visit, the things you do, and the people you meet. Then, let these ideas and impressions become the inspiration for decorating a variety of objects, including a bumper sticker, a crest, a poster, a puzzle, a shopping bag, a T-shirt, a vacation van, a visor, and more.

PUZZLES AND GAMES

Pages in the Puzzles and Games section will keep you busy when you must stay in one place and need something to do. They include codes to crack, mazes to find your way through, mysteries to solve, mathemagical squares to fill, and lists of objects to search for and find. You can work these puzzles and play these games in any order. Each one can be enjoyed alone or shared with a friend.

JOURNAL PAGES AND KEEPSAKES

The Journal Pages and Keepsakes section provides you with a place to keep the tangible mementos and intangible memories from your trip. Write your thoughts and feelings on the lines. Glue in those ticket stubs and photos. Ask someone special for an autograph. Then draw a picture or two. It's yours to create and do, and it is all up to you.

The Travel Bug helps you get ready, makes it more fun to go, and lets you keep the best parts of any trip forever.

Contents

PREPARATIONS AND IMPRESSIONS 7-58

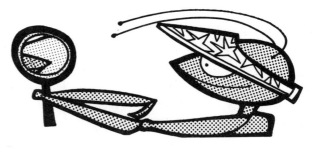

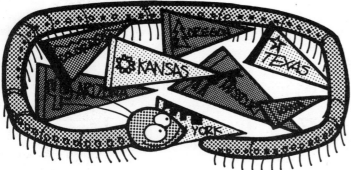

THE TRAVEL BUG
© 1993 — The Learning Works, Inc.

Contents
(continued)

PUZZLES
AND
GAMES
59-94

Contents
(continued)

THE TRAVEL BUG
© 1993 — The Learning Works, Inc.

PREPARATIONS AND IMPRESSIONS

Getting Ready to Travel

Here is a list of things to do when you and your family are getting ready to travel. Divide these responsibilities among family members who are old enough to see that they are carried out. Place a check mark in the box beside each item after it has been done.

☐ Tell trusted neighbors, the police, or the sheriff when you are leaving and how long you will be gone. Ask them to keep an eye on your house.

☐ Give a family member or friend a copy of your travel itinerary and tell this person how you can be reached in case of an emergency.

☐ If you plan to camp out or to travel abroad, check with your doctor regarding specific health risks and what precautions you should take.

☐ Refill prescriptions and purchase any medications you might need.

☐ Water all houseplants thoroughly and, if necessary, arrange for them to be watered while you are gone.

☐ Arrange for the care and feeding of all household pets.

☐ Cancel newspaper subscriptions or ask a neighbor to collect the papers each day.

☐ Notify the postal service that you will be gone and request that mail delivery be stopped, or ask a neighbor to collect and hold your mail until you return.

☐ Tell your teachers about your trip and ask them to give you the assignments for the days you will be gone.

☐ Notify coaches of the practices and games you will miss.

☐ Cancel any lessons that are scheduled or any appointments that have been made for the time that you will be away.

☐ On page 120 in this book, list the addresses of family members and friends you may want to write to while you are gone.

☐ Use the checklists on pages 9 through 11 to make certain that you pack everything you need.

☐ Travel safely and have a good trip!

THE TRAVEL BUG
© 1993 — The Learning Works, Inc.

Clothing Checklist

Use this checklist to make packing easier. Ask Mom or Dad to go through the list with you and help you decide how many of each item you will need. Write these quantities on the lines provided. Check off each item as you lay it out for packing or place it in your suitcase.

☐	0	dresses	☑	1	nightgowns/pajamas	☐	___	belts
☐	0	skirts	☐	___	robe	☐	___	caps/hats
☐	0	blouses	☐	___	slippers	☐	___	gloves/mittens
☐	0	pants (dress)	☐	___	camisoles	☐	___	boots
☐	0	pants (casual)	☐	___	slips	☐	___	shoes (dress)
☑	1	jeans	4	✓	panties/briefs	☐	___	shoes (casual)
☐	0	shirts (long-sleeved)	☐	___	undershorts	☑	1	sneakers
☑	6	shirts (short-sleeved)	☐	___	undershirts	☑	1	sandals
☑	3	shorts	☐	___	sweaters	☐	___	thongs/shower shoes
☐	___	T-shirts	☐	___	jacket (lightweight)	☐	___	socks (dress)
☑	1	sweatshirts	☐	___	jacket (heavy)	5	✓	socks (athletic)
☑	1	sweatpants	☐	___	sport coats/blazers	☐	___	hose/tights
☐	___	swimsuits	☐	___	raincoat	☐	___	scarves
☐	___	coverups	☐	___	overcoat	☐	___	ties
☐	___	_____	☐	___	_____	☐	___	umbrella
☐	___	_____	☐	___	_____	☐	___	_____

Toiletries Checklist

Use this checklist to help you remember to pack the personal and toiletry items you might otherwise forget. Check off each item as you set it out for packing or place it in your cosmetic case.

- ☐ comb
- ☐ brush
- ☐ shampoo
- ☐ setting gel
- ☐ hair spray
- ☐ hair dryer
- ☐ soap
- ☐ soap dish
- ☐ _____
- ☐ _____

- ☐ toothbrush
- ☐ toothbrush holder
- ☐ toothpaste
- ☐ deodorant
- ☐ lip balm
- ☐ sunscreen
- ☐ _____
- ☐ _____
- ☐ _____
- ☐ _____

- ☐ emery board
- ☐ fingernail clippers
- ☐ dental floss
- ☐ facial tissue
- ☐ cotton balls
- ☐ adhesive bandages
- ☐ first aid kit
- ☐ medications
- ☐ _____
- ☐ _____

THE TRAVEL BUG
© 1993 — The Learning Works, Inc.

Don't Forget to Bring

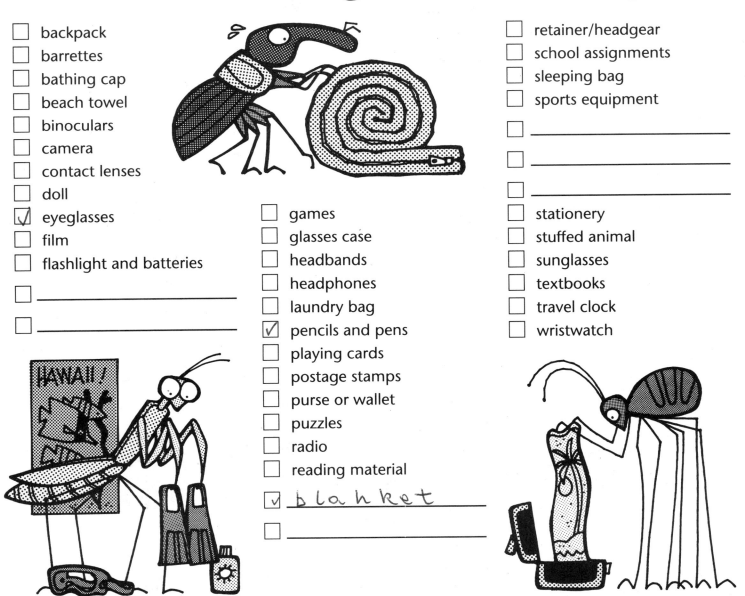

- [ ] backpack
- [ ] barrettes
- [ ] bathing cap
- [ ] beach towel
- [ ] binoculars
- [ ] camera
- [ ] contact lenses
- [ ] doll
- [x] eyeglasses
- [ ] film
- [ ] flashlight and batteries
- [ ] _____
- [ ] _____

- [ ] games
- [ ] glasses case
- [ ] headbands
- [ ] headphones
- [ ] laundry bag
- [x] pencils and pens
- [ ] playing cards
- [ ] postage stamps
- [ ] purse or wallet
- [ ] puzzles
- [ ] radio
- [ ] reading material
- [x] blanket
- [ ] _____

- [ ] retainer/headgear
- [ ] school assignments
- [ ] sleeping bag
- [ ] sports equipment
- [ ] _____
- [ ] _____
- [ ] _____
- [ ] stationery
- [ ] stuffed animal
- [ ] sunglasses
- [ ] textbooks
- [ ] travel clock
- [ ] wristwatch

Consider Collecting

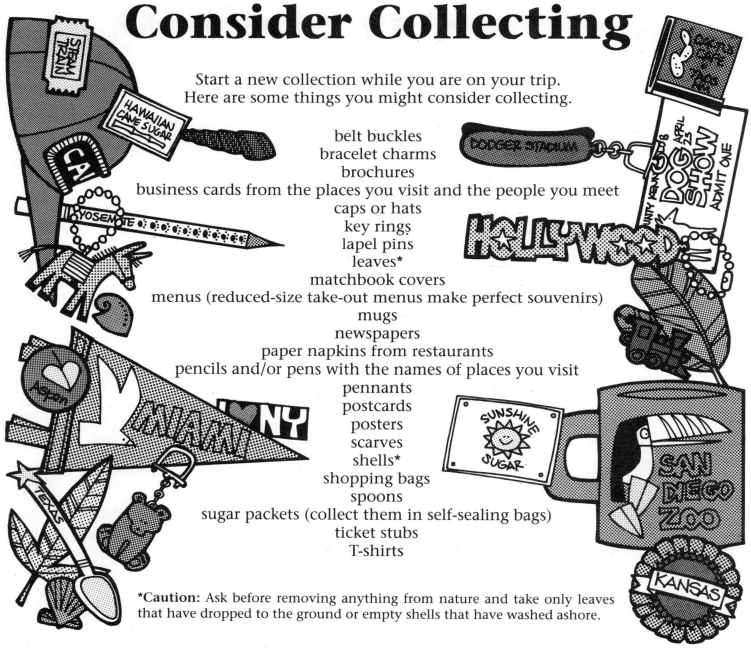

Start a new collection while you are on your trip.
Here are some things you might consider collecting.

belt buckles
bracelet charms
brochures
business cards from the places you visit and the people you meet
caps or hats
key rings
lapel pins
leaves*
matchbook covers
menus (reduced-size take-out menus make perfect souvenirs)
mugs
newspapers
paper napkins from restaurants
pencils and/or pens with the names of places you visit
pennants
postcards
posters
scarves
shells*
shopping bags
spoons
sugar packets (collect them in self-sealing bags)
ticket stubs
T-shirts

*Caution: Ask before removing anything from nature and take only leaves
that have dropped to the ground or empty shells that have washed ashore.

THE TRAVEL BUG
© 1993 — The Learning Works, Inc.

The Day I Left

I left on _Monday July 19 1999_ at _10:20_ AM .
(day, month, date, and year)   (time)

I was careful to pack my _blanket_
_____ and to _eat and drink_
_____ before I left.

I traveled with _Mom DAD PaPa ~~XXX~~ xyl_
(names of traveling companions)

_____
(names of traveling companions)

Our destination was _Cape cod_ ,
where we planned to _swim — Go To factory — walk_
on dunes — go in Tower — see ocean
(List some of the things you planned to see and do.)
go To penny patch

We traveled by (check all that apply)

- [ ] airplane
- [ ] boat
- [ ] bus
- [x] car
- [ ] foot
- [ ] helicopter
- [ ] shuttle
- [ ] subway
- [ ] taxi
- [ ] train
- [ ] _____
- [ ] _____

I hated to leave _the nice trees_ behind, but
I had heard a lot about _this Tower_
and was really looking forward to _climb it_
_____

Packed and Ready to Go!

First, draw a picture in the frame to show how you looked when you left on your trip. Then, write a caption for your picture on the lines below it.

THE TRAVEL BUG
© 1993 — The Learning Works, Inc.

State the Facts

I visited a city called _____

located in the state of _____ .

This state was admitted to the Union in _____

and thus became the _____ state.

The state I visited is bounded

     on the north by _____ ,

     on the south by _____ ,

     on the east by _____ ,

     and on the west by _____ .

The capital of this state is _____ .

Compared to my home state of _____ ,

the state I visited is

     ☐ larger   ☐ smaller   ☐ about the same size.

The state I visited is nicknamed _____

_____ .

Its motto is _____ .

This state is famous for _____

_____ .

Make a Map

In the large box below, draw the outline of a state you visited. Add the following items:

- a star and the name of the capital city in its proper place,
- circles and the names of two other important cities in their approximate locations, and
- some notable physical features, such as rivers, lakes, mountains, and deserts.

In the smaller boxes, draw and color pictures of the state flag and the state flower.

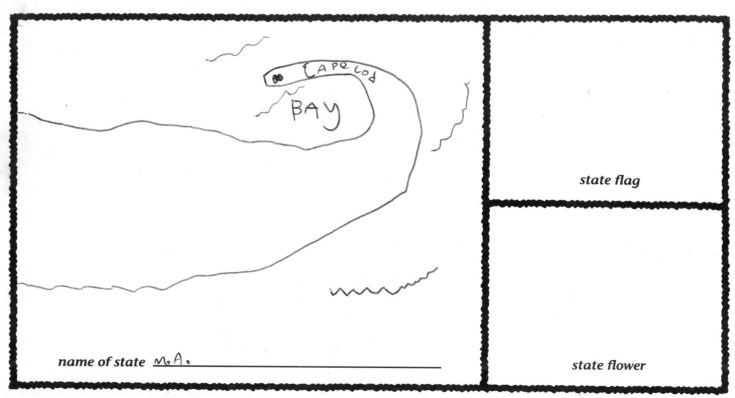

CAPE COD

BAY

name of state M. A. _____

state flag

state flower

x

16

THE TRAVEL BUG
© 1993 — The Learning Works, Inc.

Headlines & Newsmakers

HURRY & READ ALL ABOUT IT

On _____ ,
(day, month, date, and year)

I stayed at a place called _____ ,
(city, campground, park, or resort)

located in the state of _____ .

The weather was _____

_____ .

One event that received a lot of local news coverage was

_____

_____ .

An event that made headlines statewide was _____

_____

_____ .

At the same time, national newscasters were talking about

_____

_____ .

Meanwhile, back in my home state _____

_____ .

And in my hometown, _____

_____ .

HURRY & READ ALL ABOUT IT

City Scoop

On _____ ,
(day, month, date, and year)

I visited a city named _____ .

I came here to _____ .

One of the ways in which this city is like my hometown is

_____ .

One of the ways in which this city is different from my

hometown is _____ .

My instant impressions of this city are as follows:

Weather _____

Food _____

Buildings _____

Streets/Traffic _____

Parks/Open Space _____

People _____

Prices _____

Things to Do _____

Things to See _____

Thing I Liked Best _____

THE TRAVEL BUG
© 1993 — The Learning Works, Inc.

 # Museums I Visited

While traveling, I visited the following types of displays, exhibits, and museums (check all that apply):

☐ air & space   ☐ circus   ☐ memorial
☐ aquarium   ☐ dinosaur   ☐ motion picture
☐ arboretum   ☐ doll & toy   ☐ natural history
☐ archival   ☐ fashion & costume   ☐ radio & television
☐ armaments   ☐ gadget & invention ☐ science
☐ art   ☑ historical   ☐ sports
☐ automotive   ☐ industrial   ☐ transportation
☐ botanic   ☐ maritime   ☐ other _____

My favorite was the _____,
(name)

located in _____.
(city and state)

I liked it because _____
_____.

One thing I learned was that _____
_____.

After seeing it, I wish that _____
_____.

Someone Special I Met

While on my trip I met someone special named _____

_____ .

This person was a _____ .

We met while _____

_____ .

Together we _____

_____ .

We talked about _____

_____ .

This person said, " _____

_____ . "

We both enjoyed _____

_____ .

From this special person I learned _____

_____

_____ .

20

THE TRAVEL BUG
© 1993 — The Learning Works, Inc.

Create a Crest

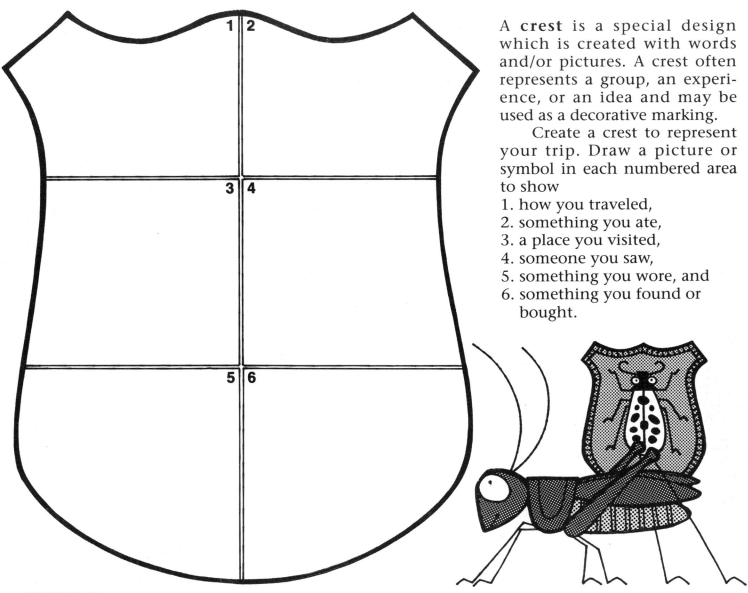

A **crest** is a special design which is created with words and/or pictures. A crest often represents a group, an experience, or an idea and may be used as a decorative marking.

Create a crest to represent your trip. Draw a picture or symbol in each numbered area to show
1. how you traveled,
2. something you ate,
3. a place you visited,
4. someone you saw,
5. something you wore, and
6. something you found or bought.

THE TRAVEL BUG
© 1993 — The Learning Works, Inc.

A Super Day

On the lines below, write about a super something that happened on the very best day of your trip.

_____

_____

_____

_____

_____

_____

_____

_____

_____

_____

_____

_____

_____

_____

_____

THE TRAVEL BUG
© 1993 — The Learning Works, Inc.

Journey Jigsaw

Think about something special that you have done on your trip. Draw a picture of it in the box below. When you get home, photocopy your picture. Use colored pencils, felt-tipped pens, or crayons to color the copy. Glue the colored copy to a piece of lightweight cardboard. Carefully cut the pieces apart. Invite a friend to work your puzzle and hear about your travels.

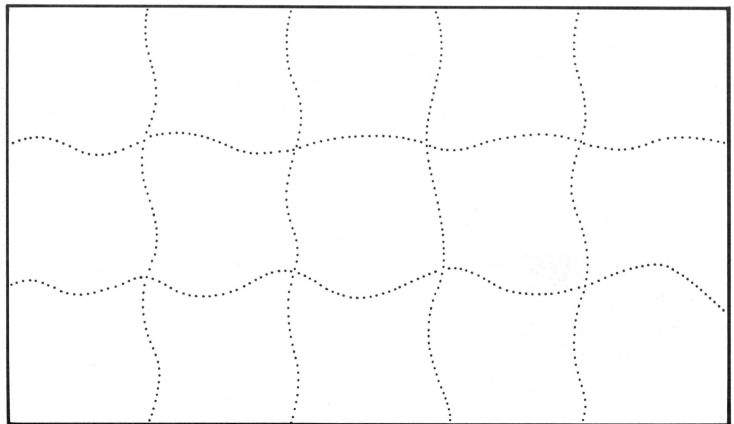

Amusement Park Superlatives

On _____ ,
(day, month, date, and year)

I visited a city called _____ ,

the home of an amusement park named _____ .

I spent about _____ hours at this park. I rode on

_____ different rides. I would rate them as follows:
(number)

Fastest _____

Slowest _____

Longest _____

Shortest _____

Noisiest _____

Quietest _____

Most Frightening _____

Most Thrilling _____

Most Entertaining _____

Most Unusual _____

Most Boring _____

Most Popular _____

My Favorite _____

24

THE TRAVEL BUG
© 1993 — The Learning Works, Inc.

Dream Up a Ride

Dream up a new ride for an amusement or theme park. Think about fun, safety, visual appeal, and the sizes and ages of the riders. Draw and color your ride in the space below. Then give it a catchy name.

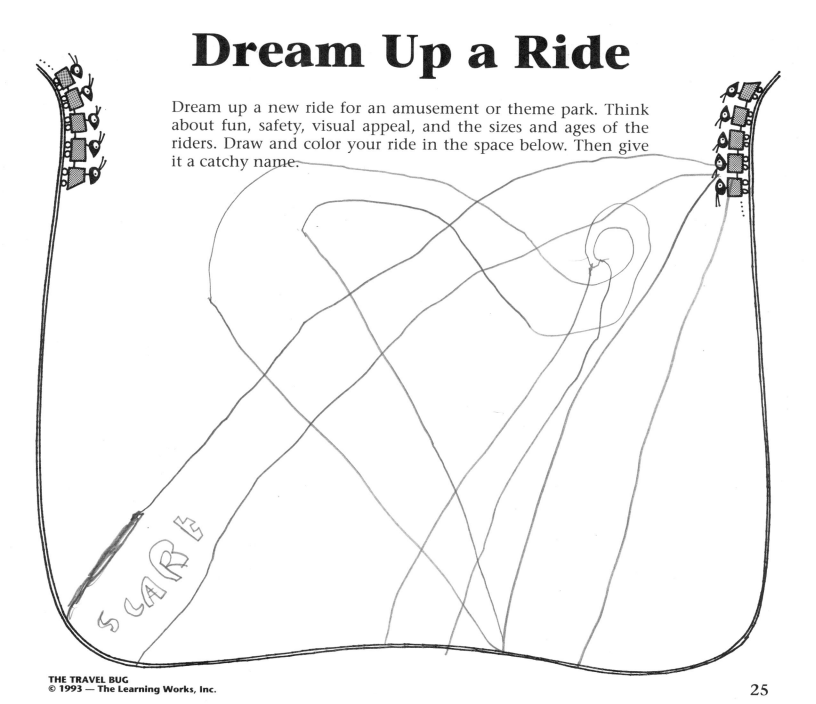

SCARE

A Tour I Took

On _____ July 22 1999 Thursday_____,
(day, month, date, and year)

I visited a city called _____ hyannis_____,

where I took a guided tour of _____ Cape Cod potato chip_____
_____ self   factory_____. *

This place was built or established in _____ ?????? _____
(year)

by _____

to _____.

It is interesting or important because _____ ThE chips_____
_____ are The best #1000 0000_____.

During the tour, I saw _____ Them rakeing chips_____

_____.

In addition, I learned that _____ They have mini_____
_____ bags_____

_____.

The most interesting thing about this place is _____

_____.

*Note: On these lines write the name of a public building, factory, garden, historical site, home, landmark, library, mansion, movie or television studio, museum, national park, or special collection you toured and a few words to identify or describe it.

THE TRAVEL BUG
© 1993 — The Learning Works, Inc.

Design a Visor

Pretend that one place you visited has selected you to design a visor to advertise this tourist attraction. First, think about what you liked about this place. Then, draw and color a visor that will make other people want to go there.

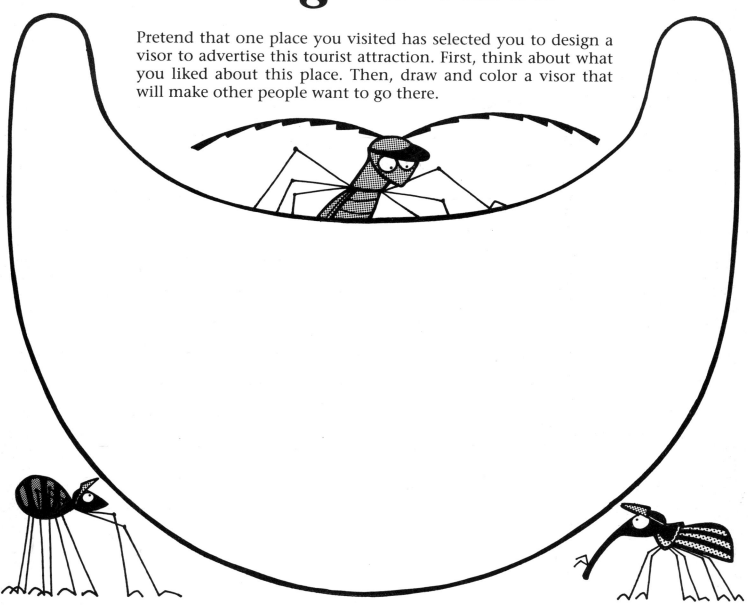

THE TRAVEL BUG
© 1993 — The Learning Works, Inc.

Movie Review

A movie I saw during my trip was _____

_____ .

This movie starred _____

_____ .

It was about _____

_____

_____ .

My favorite part of the movie was when _____

_____

_____

_____ .

I would rate this movie as follows (circle the number):

1 So boring that I did not watch all of it.

2 Worth the time only if you have nothing else to do.

3 Okay once but definitely not twice.

4 Worth recommending to friends.

5 One of the best I have ever seen and well worth seeing again!

THE TRAVEL BUG
© 1993 — The Learning Works, Inc.

Movie Review

Draw a picture of your favorite part of the movie in the space below.

Visiting History

One historical site I visited was _____
_____ .

It is located _____
_____ .

This site is important because _____
_____
_____ .

That event took place in the year _____ .

An important person associated with this site is _____
_____ .

He or she _____
_____ .

The most interesting thing I learned about this site is _____
_____
_____ .

When I tell my friends about my trip, I will say that this site
_____
_____ .

THE TRAVEL BUG
© 1993 — The Learning Works, Inc.

Visiting History

Draw a picture of a historical site you visited in the space below.

Pilgrim monument

Nature Scavenger Hunt

Go on a nature walk. Look for these things. Put an **x** in the box beside each one that you find.

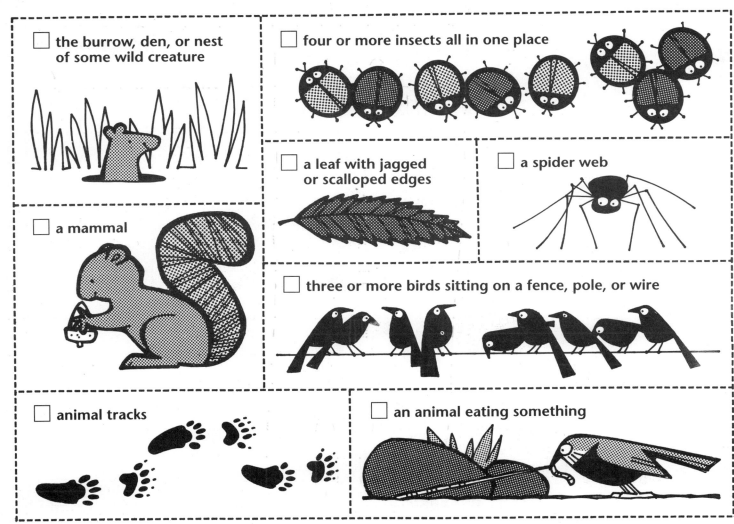

☐ the burrow, den, or nest of some wild creature

☐ four or more insects all in one place

☐ a mammal

☐ a leaf with jagged or scalloped edges

☐ a spider web

☐ three or more birds sitting on a fence, pole, or wire

☐ animal tracks

☐ an animal eating something

THE TRAVEL BUG
© 1993 — The Learning Works, Inc.

Eyes on the Environment

While you are traveling, notice how well one of the cities you visit protects the environment. Compare this city with your hometown by putting check marks in the appropriate boxes.

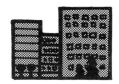

| City Visited | | Signs of a Healthy Environment | My Hometown | |
Yes	No		Yes	No
		Has plenty of clear, fresh water in lakes, streams, and/or reservoirs		
		Has clear, pure air and policies to keep it that way		
		Provides protected areas for plants and animals		
		Keeps most public buildings freshly painted and free of graffiti		
		Has ample public parks and open spaces and maintains them in safe, usable condition		
		Keeps sidewalks and streets safe, clean, and free of litter		
		Provides sufficient trash cans for litter and empties them regularly		
		Encourages recycling and even offers a curbside recycling program		

Note: Most of these questions can be answered by observation. If you need additional information, talk to friends, relatives, and other people who live in the city you are visiting.

Sensational Statistics

Statistics are numbers that tell how old, how big, how high, how deep, how wide, how far, how fast, how much, how many, and/or how often. As you travel, collect some statistics about the places you visit. Record six of your most sensational statistics on the lines below.

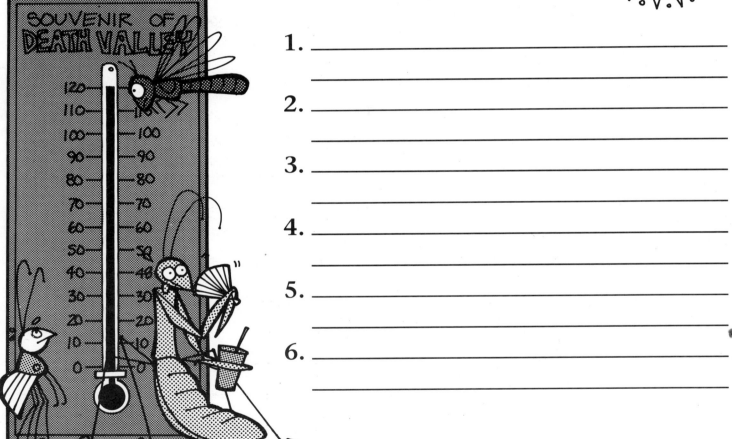

1. _____

_____

2. _____

_____

3. _____

_____

4. _____

_____

5. _____

_____

6. _____

_____

THE TRAVEL BUG
© 1993 — The Learning Works, Inc.

Fabulous Five

On _____ ,
(day, month, date, and year)

I spent the day in _____ ,
(city and state)

where I enjoyed visiting and/or watching a/an

- [ ] amusement park
- [ ] aquarium
- [ ] beach
- [ ] carnival
- [ ] collection
- [ ] concert

- [ ] factory
- [ ] festival
- [ ] game
- [ ] garden
- [ ] house or mansion
- [ ] museum

- [ ] parade
- [ ] park
- [ ] planetarium
- [ ] play
- [ ] rodeo
- [ ] zoo

- [ ] other _____

Of these, my favorite was _____ .
(full name)

The five most fun, interesting, or exciting things I saw, heard, and/or did there are:

1. _____

2. _____

3. _____

4. _____

5. _____

A Hilarious Happening

A funny thing happened to me while I was away on vacation.

It was about _____ on _____ .
(time)   (day and/or month and date)

We were in _____ ,
(where you were at the time)

and I was _____ .
(what you were doing)

Suddenly, _____
(the first thing that happened)

_____ .

The next thing I knew, _____
(the next thing that happened)

_____ .

I _____
(how you reacted and/or what you tried to do)

_____ ,

but _____

_____ .

Then, _____

_____ .

It all ended when _____

_____

_____ .

THE TRAVEL BUG
© 1993 — The Learning Works, Inc.

Plan a Poster

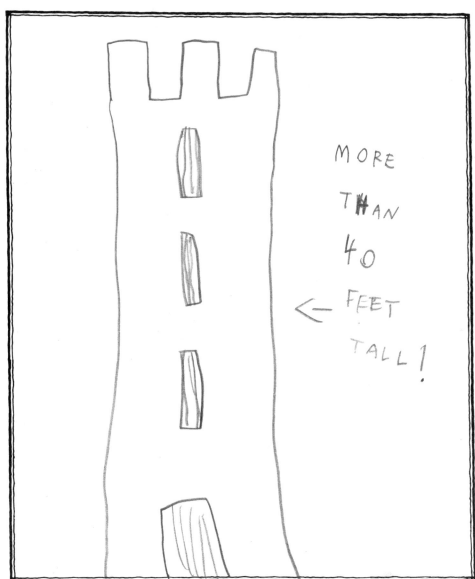

MORE THAN 40 ← FEET TALL!

A **poster** is an advertisement, bill, or notice intended for display in a public place. Poster artists use colors, pictures, and words in eye-catching ways to convey their messages. These messages may be about a person, a place, an event, or an idea.

In this space, create a mini-poster — or **handbill** — to advertise a person you met, a place you visited, or an event you attended while on your trip or to explain an idea you feel strongly about because of something you saw or did while traveling.

Fabulous Travel Firsts

Recall some of the things that you did for the first time during your trip. Then write a word or phrase on each line.

This trip was *the first time that*

I traveled by _____

I experienced being 252 feet

I tried to _____

I played a game of _____

I watched _____

I heard _____

I saw great sceanary

I smelled _____

I tasted lobster

I felt _____

I met _____

I visited _____

I collected _____

I discovered _____

I enjoyed _____

THE TRAVEL BUG
© 1993 — The Learning Works, Inc.

Create a Menu Cover

A **menu** is a list of the food items that may be ordered in a restaurant or of the dishes that will be served during a banquet or other special meal.

Think of a restaurant in which you ate while traveling. Use pictures, words, and colors to create a new cover for this restaurant's menu.

Pen a Postcard

Draw and color a postcard-perfect picture of a place you visited or something you saw on your trip. Write a matching message on page 41.

THE TRAVEL BUG
© 1993 — The Learning Works, Inc.

Pen a Postcard

Write a message about something special you saw or did. Address the postcard to someone with whom you would like to share this travel adventure. Design your own postage stamp.

_____

_____ ,

_____

_____

_____   _____

_____   _____

_____   _____

_____   _____

_____

_____ ,

_____

message   *address*

Number, Please

Just for fun, think about your trip in terms of meals, miles, minutes, money, and more. On each line below, write the number that applies.

The number of miles you traveled on the longest day of your trip   ——————— miles

The number of meals you ate at fast food restaurants   ——————— meals

The number of steps you took to get from your parked vehicle to your motel room, cabin, or campsite   ——————— steps

The total number of relatives you met, saw, or talked with   ——————— relatives

The number of times you slept on the ground or floor   ——————— times

The number of stories in the tallest building you saw   ——————— stories

The largest number of minutes you waited in line to buy a meal, take a tour, or see a show   ——————— minutes

The number of things you left behind, lost, or forgot   ——————— things

The number of letters you wrote   ——————— letters

The number of postcards you sent   ——————— postcards

The number of souvenirs you collected   ——————— souvenirs

The total amount of money you spent   ———————————

THE TRAVEL BUG
© 1993 — The Learning Works, Inc.

T Is for Travel

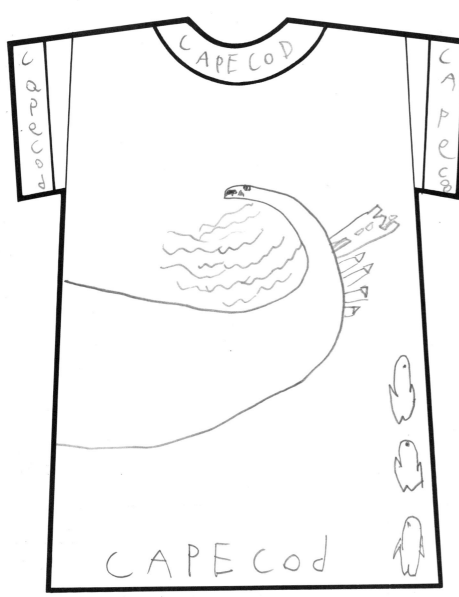

Design a T-shirt to represent some place you visited, something you saw, something you did, or something you learned while on vacation. When you get home, consider duplicating your design on an actual T-shirt using fabric or puff paints.

Bumper Sticker Fun

Bumper stickers can be used to express ideas about everything from politics to pets. As you travel, notice bumper stickers. Copy one of your favorites here.

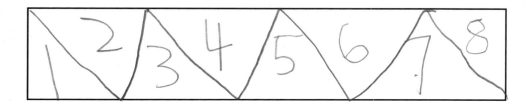

Create two more bumper stickers in the boxes below. Remember to keep the messages short and to the point so that people passing by will be able to understand them at a glance.

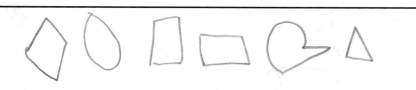

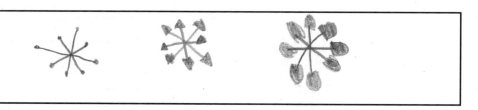

44

THE TRAVEL BUG
© 1993 — The Learning Works, Inc.

A Diamonte or Two

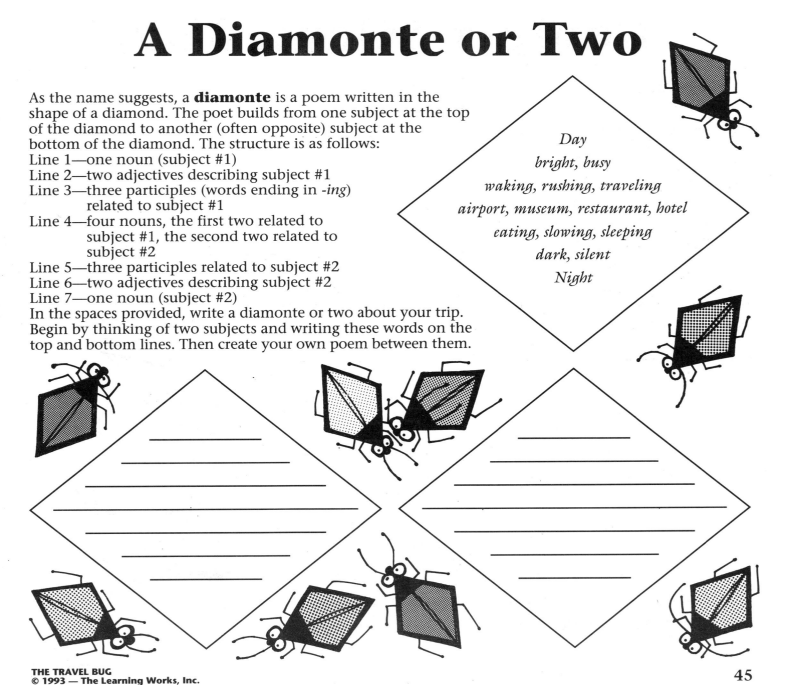

As the name suggests, a **diamonte** is a poem written in the shape of a diamond. The poet builds from one subject at the top of the diamond to another (often opposite) subject at the bottom of the diamond. The structure is as follows:

Line 1—one noun (subject #1)
Line 2—two adjectives describing subject #1
Line 3—three participles (words ending in -*ing*)
    related to subject #1
Line 4—four nouns, the first two related to
    subject #1, the second two related to
    subject #2
Line 5—three participles related to subject #2
Line 6—two adjectives describing subject #2
Line 7—one noun (subject #2)

In the spaces provided, write a diamonte or two about your trip. Begin by thinking of two subjects and writing these words on the top and bottom lines. Then create your own poem between them.

Day
bright, busy
waking, rushing, traveling
airport, museum, restaurant, hotel
eating, slowing, sleeping
dark, silent
Night

A Poem About a Place

1. Choose a place you visited on your trip or vacation.
2. Print the name of this place in capital letters on the lines below. As you print the name, place each letter under the one before it.
3. Use each letter to begin a line that tells something about this place or something you learned while you were there.
4. The lines do not need to rhyme.

Example: **M** ighty mastadons marched
      U ntil
      S omething made them
      E xtinct,
      U ntil
      M orning came and they were no more.

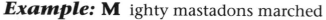

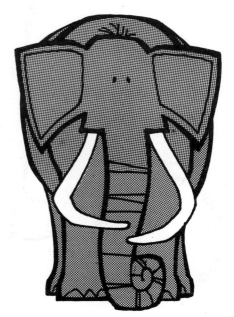

46

Customize a Vacation Van

While you are traveling, notice family, service, and delivery vans. Then customize this van so that it becomes an ideal vacation vehicle.

Personalize a Plate

Some states permit vehicle owners to personalize their license plates with a special motto or message. Use combinations of letters and numbers to create personalized licenses in the plates below. Put no more than seven letters and/or numbers on any one plate.

Example:

1 0 S A N Y 1

(Tennis, anyone?)

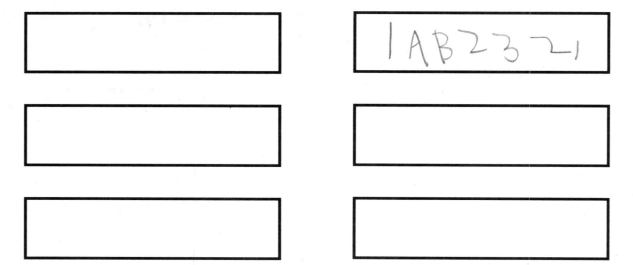

1 A B 2 3 2 1

THE TRAVEL BUG
© 1993 — The Learning Works, Inc.

The I-N-G Me

On each line, write one word that ends in the letters **i-n-g** and names something you enjoyed doing on your trip. In each box, draw a picture of you doing the thing that word names.

hiking   sailing   eating

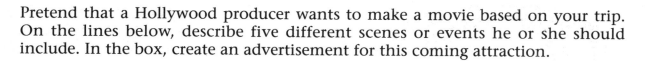

Making a Movie

Pretend that a Hollywood producer wants to make a movie based on your trip. On the lines below, describe five different scenes or events he or she should include. In the box, create an advertisement for this coming attraction.

1. _____
   _____
   _____

2. _____
   _____
   _____

3. _____
   _____
   _____

4. _____
   _____
   _____

5. _____
   _____
   _____

THE TRAVEL BUG
© 1993 — The Learning Works, Inc.

Bag Bonanza

Notice the decorative shopping bags that museums, restaurants, and stores use as advertisements. In this space, create a bag to advertise one of the following sights or sites:

amusement park
beach or shore
camp or campground
dude ranch
hiking trail
historical monument
hot dog stand
hotel or motel
lakeside setting
mountain resort
museum
national park
restaurant
ski lift
souvenir shop
sporting goods store
waterfall
wilderness area

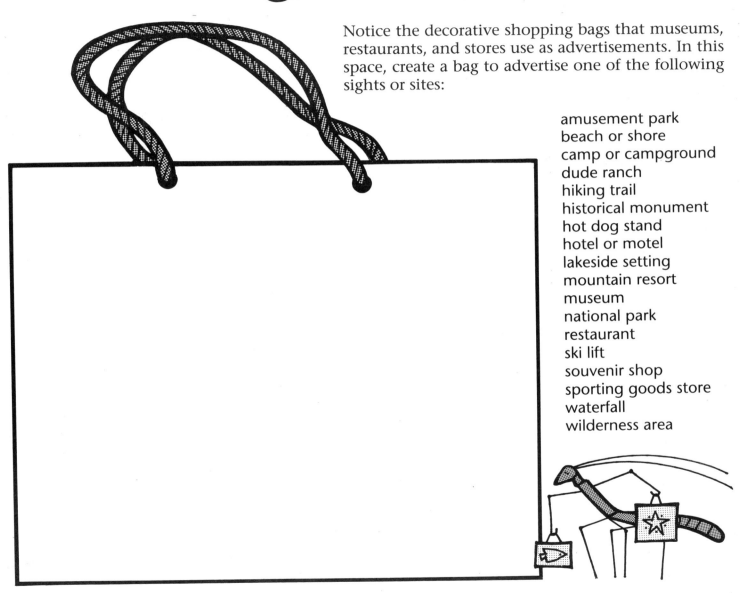

Who's in the Zoo?

If you visit a zoo during your vacation, look for animals to match these descriptions. Put an **x** in the box beside each one you find. Then write the name of the animal on the line.

- [ ] a baby animal _____
- [ ] an animal with feathers _____
- [ ] an animal with fur _____
- [ ] an animal with scales _____
- [ ] a black-and-white animal _____
- [ ] an animal with stripes _____
- [ ] an animal that lives on land _____
- [ ] an animal that lives in water _____
- [ ] an animal that lives in a tree _____
- [ ] an animal that lays eggs _____
- [ ] a noisy animal _____
- [ ] a quiet animal _____
- [ ] an animal that would fit in your hand _____
- [ ] your favorite animal _____

THE TRAVEL BUG
© 1993 — The Learning Works, Inc.

More Who's in the Zoo?

If you visit a zoo during your vacation, look for animals to match these descriptions. Put an **x** in the box beside each one you find. Then write the name of the animal on the line.

- [ ] a reptile
- [ ] an amphibian
- [ ] a carnivore
- [ ] a herbivore
- [ ] an omnivore
- [ ] a nocturnal animal
- [ ] a pit viper
- [ ] a nonpoisonous snake
- [ ] a warm-blooded animal
- [ ] a cold-blooded animal
- [ ] a desert animal
- [ ] a forest animal
- [ ] an endangered animal
- [ ] an Arctic animal
- [ ] an animal native to Asia
- [ ] an animal native to Australia
- [ ] a South American animal
- [ ] an animal that ruminates
- [ ] the animal you most like to watch

_____
_____
_____
_____
_____
_____
_____
_____
_____
_____
_____
_____
_____
_____
_____
_____
_____
_____
_____

Shade a Shape

Shade each shape with an even number in it to discover one way to travel.

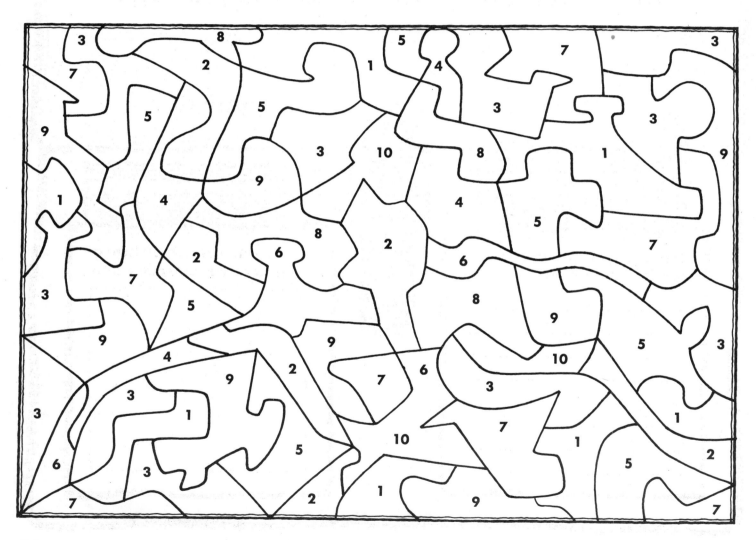

54

THE TRAVEL BUG
© 1993 — The Learning Works, Inc.

Best Book Backpack

What was the best book you read on your trip?

Title _____

Author _____

☐ Fiction or ☐ Nonfiction

NOTES

Describe your favorite part on the lines below.

_____
_____
_____
_____
_____
_____
_____
_____

THE ADVENTURES OF

Name and draw a picture of your favorite character here.

Create a Billboard

As you travel, notice the billboards. Most billboard messages are short and to the point because people riding by in vehicles have only a few seconds in which to read them. Think of a tourist attraction you visited while on your trip. Create a billboard to advertise this attraction. Use no more than ten words in your message. Be sure to include a drawing. Color it with crayons, colored pencils, or felt-tipped pens.

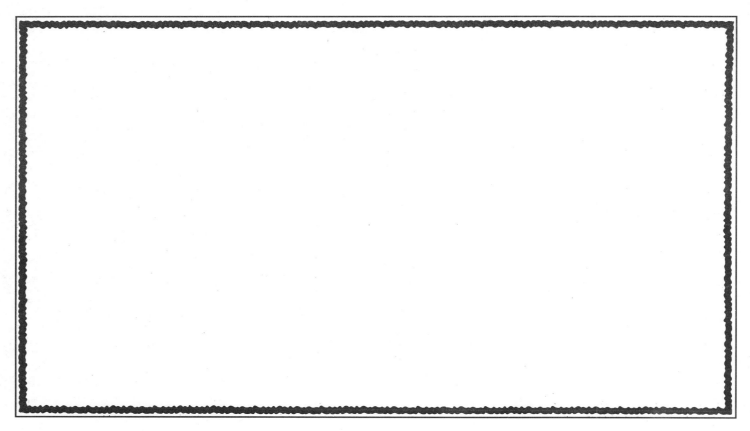

THE TRAVEL BUG
© 1993 — The Learning Works, Inc.

Looking Back

I returned on _____ at _____ .
(day, month, date, and year)   (time)

After being gone _____ days and _____ hours,

it felt _____ to be home again!

Looking back, the two things I enjoyed most about my trip

were _____

_____ .

The thing I liked least was _____

_____ .

The funniest thing that happened was _____

_____ .

One interesting thing I learned while on my trip was that

_____

_____ .

The one thing I'll always remember about this trip is _____

_____ .

One thing I would do differently next time is _____

_____ .

Happy to Be Home Again!

First, draw a picture in the frame to show how you looked on the day you returned home after your trip or vacation. Next, write a caption for your picture on the lines below. Then, just for fun, compare this picture with the one you drew of yourself on page 14, before you went traveling.

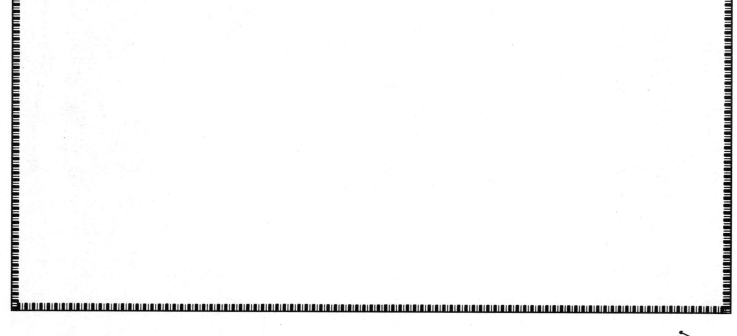

THE TRAVEL BUG
© 1993 — The Learning Works, Inc.

PUZZLES
AND
GAMES

The Alphabet Game

Find a word that begins with each letter of the alphabet. Start with the letter **A** and go *in order*. Look for words on benches, billboards, buildings, and signs — anywhere outside the vehicle in which you are traveling. Write each word below. If you are unable to find words that begin with **X** and **Z**, list words in which these letters appear.

TRUCKS

YOGURT

A _____

B _____

C _____

D _____

E _____

F _____

G _____

H _____

I _____

J _____

K _____

L _____

M _____

N _____

O _____

P _____

Q _____

R _____

S _____

T _____

U _____

V _____

W _____

X _____

Y _____

Z _____

LOCK

CIRCUS

HOURLY

GOLF

TACOS

FOREST

FAX

FAIR

MOTEL

PORT

CANYON

SKI

THE TRAVEL BUG
© 1993 — The Learning Works, Inc.

The Alphabet Game

Find a word that begins with each letter of the alphabet. Start with the letter **A** and go *in order*. Look for words on benches, billboards, buildings, and signs — anywhere outside the vehicle in which you are traveling. Write each word below. If you are unable to find words that begin with **X** and **Z**, list words in which these letters appear.

A _____ J _____ R _____

B _____ K _____ S _____

C _____ L _____ T _____

D _____ M _____ U _____

E _____ N _____ V _____

F _____ O _____ W _____

G _____ P _____ X _____

H _____ Q _____ Y _____

I _____   Z _____

CAVERNS **HORSE** **KARATE**
SHOPS **LUGGAGE** MUSEUM
PARKING **ICY** AQUARIUM

The Alphabet Game

Find a word that begins with each letter of the alphabet. Start with the letter **A** and go *in order*. Look for words on benches, billboards, buildings, and signs — anywhere outside the vehicle in which you are traveling. Write each word below. If you are unable to find words that begin with **X** and **Z**, list words in which these letters appear.

A _____   J _____   R _____

B _____   K _____   S _____

C _____   L _____   T _____

D _____   M _____   U _____

E _____   N _____   V _____

F _____   O _____   W _____

G _____   P _____   X _____

H _____   Q _____   Y _____

I _____   Z _____

QUIET

HOT DOGS   **REDWOOD**   **SURF**

TENNIS   **VIDEOS**

INN   RANCH   **HILLS**   **BEACH**

THE TRAVEL BUG
© 1993 — The Learning Works, Inc.

The Alphabet Game

Find a word that begins with each letter of the alphabet. Start with the letter **A** and go *in order*. Look for words on benches, billboards, buildings, and signs — anywhere outside the vehicle in which you are traveling. Write each word below. If you are unable to find words that begin with **X** and **Z**, list words in which these letters appear.

A _____   J _____   R _____

B _____   K _____   S _____

C _____   L _____   T _____

D _____   M _____   U _____

E _____   N _____   V _____

F _____   O _____   W _____

G _____   P _____   X _____

H _____   Q _____   Y _____

I _____   Z _____

RIVER

STOP **CAROUSEL** **POOL** **TAXI**

BURGERS **FUDGE** **MALL**

ZOO **DEER** AIRPORT YACHTS

AUTOMOBILE Puzzle

1. See how many words of three or more letters you can make using *only* the letters in the word **automobile**.
2. You may use each letter in any word you make only the number of times that it appears in the word **automobile**.
   Example: The word **boot** is allowed because there are two **o**'s in **automobile**.
   The word **bib** is not allowed because there is only one **b** in **automobile**.
3. Names of persons and places or other proper nouns do *not* count.

A U T O M O B I L E

1. Too
2. boat
3. Mile
4. Tile
5. boot
6. Oat
7. Auto
8. Mobile
9. Boom
10. Loom
11. MOB
12. MAT
13. Tomb
14. Moat
15. BILE
16. OIL
17. BOIL
18. TOIL
19. TOOL
20. BLOOM
21.
22.
23.
24.
25.
26.
27.
28.
29.
30.

boot
pat

64

THE TRAVEL BUG
© 1993 — The Learning Works, Inc.

LOCOMOTIVE Puzzle

1. See how many words of three or more letters you can make using *only* the letters in the word **locomotive**.
2. You may use each letter in any word you make only the number of times that it appears in the word **locomotive**.
   Example: The word **cool** is allowed because there are at least two **o**'s in **locomotive**.
   The word **meet** is not allowed because there is only one **e** in **locomotive**.
3. Names of persons and places or other proper nouns do *not* count.

L O C O M O T I V E

1. TOO	11. COMET	21. TILE
2. MOO	12. LIVE	22. EVIL
3. COME	13. TOOL	23. EVICT
4. COVE	14. COOL	24. CLOUT
5. LOVE	15. MOVIE	25. VOTE
6. MOVE	16. TOME	26. MITE
7. MOOT	17. COOT	27. MOTE
8. CLOVE	18. LOOT	28.
9. CLOT	19. MOTIVE	29.
10. LOT	20. MILE	30.

HELICOPTER Puzzle

1. See how many words of three or more letters you can make using *only* the letters in the word **helicopter**.
2. You may use each letter in any word you make only the number of times that it appears in the word **helicopter**.
   Example: The word **there** is allowed because there are two **e**'s in **helicopter**.
   The word **hoop** is not allowed because there is only one **o** in **helicopter**.
3. Names of persons and places or other proper nouns do *not* count.

H E L I C O P T E R

1. LICE
2. Ice
3. Rice
4. Price
5. thrice
6. cope
7. cop
8. help
9. Rope
10. hope
11. chop
12. top
13. pot
14. pit
15. trip
16. tripe
17. clip
18. chip
19. Heel
20. Reel
21. peel
22. clot
23. clop
24. Lope
25. lop
26. elope
27. Pelt
28. her
29. there
30. the

THE TRAVEL BUG
© 1993 — The Learning Works, Inc.

Building Search

As you travel, see if you can spot examples of these different kinds of buildings. Look for them in any order. Put an **x** in the box beside each one you find. Mark *only one box* for each building. For example, *do not count* the same building as both a **laundry or laundromat** and a **dry cleaners**. If there is more than one player, write the finder's initial in the box. The object is to find as many of these buildings as you can before you reach your destination or run out of time. With more than one player, the winner is the one who finds the most buildings.

- [ ] bank
- [ ] barber or beauty shop
- [ ] bookstore
- [ ] bowling alley
- [ ] card and gift shop
- [ ] church, mosque, or synagogue
- [ ] department store
- [ ] drugstore or pharmacy

- [ ] dry cleaners
- [ ] furniture store
- [ ] gas station
- [ ] grocery store
- [ ] hospital
- [ ] hotel or motel
- [ ] laundry or laundromat
- [ ] library

- [ ] movie theater
- [ ] office building
- [ ] pet store
- [ ] post office
- [ ] school
- [ ] shoe store
- [ ] stationery store
- [ ] video store

Food Establishment Search

As you travel, see if you can spot examples of these establishments that sell and/or serve food. Look for them in any order. Put an **x** in the box beside each one you find. Mark *only one box* for each food establishment. *Do not count* the same place as both a **pizza kitchen** and an **Italian restaurant**. If there is more than one player, write the finder's initial in the box. The object is to find as many of these food establishments as you can before you reach your destination or run out of time. With more than one player, the winner is the one who finds the most food establishments.

☐ bakery	☐ fruit stand
☐ barbeque restaurant	☐ hamburger grill
☐ butcher shop	☐ health food store
☐ candy store	☐ ice cream shop
☐ chicken take-out	☐ Italian restaurant
☐ Chinese restaurant	☐ Japanese restaurant
☐ delicatessen	☐ Mexican restaurant
☐ donut shop	☐ pie shop
☐ drive-through restaurant	☐ pizza kitchen
☐ farmers' market	☐ sandwich shop
☐ fast food restaurant	☐ seafood restaurant
☐ fish market	☐ vegetable stand

THE TRAVEL BUG
© 1993 — The Learning Works, Inc.

People Search

As you wait in a terminal or ride on a bus, plane, or train, see if you can spot people doing these different things. Look for them in any order. Put an **x** in the box beside each one you find. Mark *only one box* for each person. For example, *do not count* the same person as both **reading a newspaper** and **doing a puzzle**. If there is more than one player, write the finder's initial in the box. The object is to find as many of these people as you can before you reach your destination or run out of time. With more than one player, the winner is the one who finds the most.

- [ ] asking for directions
- [ ] buying a ticket
- [ ] calling an attendant
- [ ] doing a puzzle
- [ ] drinking a soda
- [ ] eating a snack
- [ ] feeding a baby
- [ ] knitting or crocheting
- [ ] making a phone call
- [ ] playing a game with a child
- [ ] playing cards

- [ ] reading a book
- [ ] reading a magazine
- [ ] reading a newspaper
- [ ] reading to a child
- [ ] taking a nap
- [ ] talking with someone
- [ ] using a calculator
- [ ] using a computer
- [ ] wearing headphones
- [ ] writing
- [ ] yawning and stretching

Miscellaneous Search

As you travel, see if you can spot examples of these miscellaneous items. Look for them in any order. Put an **x** in the box beside each one you find. Mark *only one box* for each item. *Do not count* the same item as both a **call box** and a **public telephone**. If there is more than one player, write the finder's initial in the box. The object is to find as many of these items as you can before you reach your destination or run out of time. With more than one player, the winner is the one who finds the most items.

☐ athletic field or park	☐ flag
☐ bicycle	☐ for sale sign
☐ bridge	☐ historical marker
☐ call box	☐ mailbox
☐ car wash	☐ motel billboard
☐ cemetery	☐ movie marquee
☐ clock	☐ public telephone
☐ delivery truck	☐ restaurant billboard
☐ dog	☐ statue
☐ emergency vehicle	☐ swimming pool
☐ empty bus bench	☐ ticket or toll booth
☐ fire hydrant	☐ white fence

WILSON

PONY FOR SALE

70

Sign Search

As you travel, watch for these signs. Look for them in any order. Put an **x** in the box beside each one you see. Mark *only one box* for each sign. If there is more than one player, write the finder's initial in the box. The object is to find as many of these signs as you can before you reach your destination or run out of time. With more than one player, the winner is the one who finds the most signs.

stop	yield	railroad crossing	no bicycles	no trucks	no U turn
no left turn	no right turn	divided highway	merge	winding road	slippery when wet
hill	picnic area	telephone	farm machinery	cattle crossing	deer crossing

Station Search

While you are waiting in an airport, bus station, or train station, see if you can spot these items. Look for them in any order. Put an **x** in the box beside each one you find. Mark *only one box* for each item. If there is more than one player, write the finder's initial in the box. The object is to find as many of these items as you can before you reach your destination or run out of time. With more than one player, the winner is the one who finds the most items.

- [ ] baby stroller
- [ ] baggage cart
- [ ] baggage claim sign
- [ ] baggage scale
- [ ] car rental counter
- [ ] clock
- [ ] conveyor belt
- [ ] elevator
- [ ] escalator
- [ ] exit sign
- [ ] mailbox

- [ ] newspaper
- [ ] no smoking sign
- [ ] pay telephone
- [ ] person in uniform
- [ ] pet carrier
- [ ] restaurant
- [ ] restrooms
- [ ] souvenir or gift shop
- [ ] stamp machine
- [ ] trash can
- [ ] water fountain

EXIT ➡

TOYLAND

THE TRAVEL BUG
© 1993 — The Learning Works, Inc.

Truck Search

As you travel, watch for trucks. Look for them in any order. Put an **x** in the box beside each one you see. Mark *only one box* for each truck. For example, *do not count* one vehicle as both a **fire truck** and a **red truck**. If there is more than one player, write the finder's initial in the box. The object is to find as many of these trucks as you can before you reach your destination or run out of time. With more than one player, the winner is the one who finds the most trucks.

- [ ] bottle truck
- [ ] cement truck
- [ ] delivery van
- [ ] dump truck
- [ ] fire truck
- [ ] flatbed truck
- [ ] furniture truck
- [ ] garbage truck
- [ ] mail truck
- [ ] motor home

- [ ] moving van
- [ ] panel truck
- [ ] pickup truck
- [ ] platform truck
- [ ] red truck
- [ ] tractor and semitrailer
- [ ] tow truck
- [ ] yellow truck
- [ ] truck with a dog inside
- [ ] truck being driven by a woman

Twenty Category Game

As you travel, look for words that match the categories and start with the letters listed below. Write each word you find in the appropriate box. Try to fill all of the boxes before you reach your destination or run out of time.

Letters	The Name of a Restaurant	The Name of a Hotel or Motel	The Name of a Shop or Store	Any Word That You Have Not Yet Used
D				
M				
R				
S				
T				

74

Suitcase Sums

Each of these suitcases is supposed to contain a mathemagical square. In a mathemagical square, the numbers are arranged so that the sum remains the same whether you add across a row, down a column, or along a diagonal. In each of these suitcases, pack the numbers needed to complete the mathemagical square. For **Suitcase Number 1**, the sum is **24**.

Mystery in the Museum

Shortly after a tour group left the Maples Museum, a guard reported that a priceless necklace was missing. Although each person in the group denied taking the necklace, the special investigator assigned to the case reasoned that the last person to leave the museum was the culprit. Use the clues given below to discover which tour group member was the last to leave. On the line beside each name, write the time that person left the museum. Then write the name of the thief at the bottom of the page.

_____ **Barbara Baez** left twenty minutes before Betsy Bowers.

_____ **Bobby Beaver** left fifteen minutes after Ben Babbitt.

_____ **Bessie Baker** left fifty minutes before Barbara Baez.

_____ **Betsy Bowers** left thirty-five minutes after Bobby Beaver.

_____ **Bruno Bailey** left fifteen minutes before five o'clock.

_____ **Betty Blair** left twenty-five minutes after Barbara Baez.

_____ **Ben Babbitt** left twenty minutes before Bruno Bailey.

_____ **Brett Butler** left forty-five minutes before Bobby Beaver.

_____ **Bart Brown** left ten minutes before Betty Blair.

The thief was _____ .

THE TRAVEL BUG
© 1993 — The Learning Works, Inc.

The Suspects

Bobby Beaver	Bessie Baker	Barbara Baez
Betty Blair	Bart Brown	Betsy Bowers
Bruno Bailey	Ben Babbitt	Brett Butler

Wonderful Word-a-Cycle

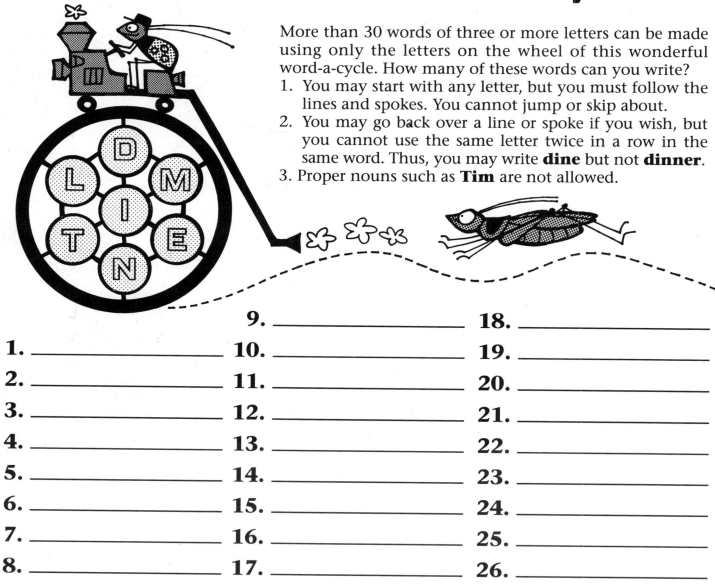

More than 30 words of three or more letters can be made using only the letters on the wheel of this wonderful word-a-cycle. How many of these words can you write?

1. You may start with any letter, but you must follow the lines and spokes. You cannot jump or skip about.
2. You may go back over a line or spoke if you wish, but you cannot use the same letter twice in a row in the same word. Thus, you may write **dine** but not **dinner**.
3. Proper nouns such as **Tim** are not allowed.

1. _____
2. _____
3. _____
4. _____
5. _____
6. _____
7. _____
8. _____
9. _____
10. _____
11. _____
12. _____
13. _____
14. _____
15. _____
16. _____
17. _____
18. _____
19. _____
20. _____
21. _____
22. _____
23. _____
24. _____
25. _____
26. _____

78

THE TRAVEL BUG
© 1993 — The Learning Works, Inc.

Word Away

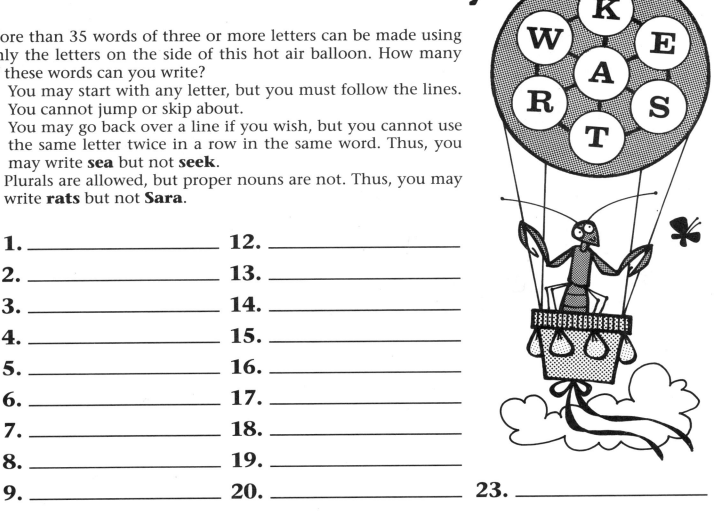

More than 35 words of three or more letters can be made using only the letters on the side of this hot air balloon. How many of these words can you write?

1. You may start with any letter, but you must follow the lines. You cannot jump or skip about.
2. You may go back over a line if you wish, but you cannot use the same letter twice in a row in the same word. Thus, you may write **sea** but not **seek**.
3. Plurals are allowed, but proper nouns are not. Thus, you may write **rats** but not **Sara**.

1. _____
2. _____
3. _____
4. _____
5. _____
6. _____
7. _____
8. _____
9. _____
10. _____
11. _____

12. _____
13. _____
14. _____
15. _____
16. _____
17. _____
18. _____
19. _____
20. _____
21. _____
22. _____

23. _____
24. _____
25. _____

Airport Dash

Marvin and Marilyn Mantis have arrived at the airport just minutes before flight time. Help them thread their way through the throng to the departure gate, where their aircraft waits.

FLIGHT 24 NOW BOARDING

GATE 5

THE TRAVEL BUG
© 1993 — The Learning Works, Inc.

Campward Bound

Bernard and Betsy Beetle have been hiking in the woods all day and are exhausted. Help them find their way back to their friends, a warm fire, a camp-cooked meal, and a good night's sleep.

License Plate Search No. 1

As you travel, look at vehicle license plates. Notice which state each plate is from. Place an **x** in the box beside each state you see. Mark them in any order, but try to find all fifty before you reach your destination or run out of time.

- [x] Alabama
- [ ] Alaska
- [x] Arizona
- [ ] Arkansas
- [x] California
- [ ] Colorado
- [x] Connecticut
- [x] Delaware
- [x] Florida
- [x] Georgia
- [ ] Hawaii
- [ ] Idaho
- [x] Illinois
- [x] Indiana
- [x] Iowa
- [ ] Kansas
- [x] Kentucky

- [ ] Louisiana
- [x] Maine
- [x] Maryland
- [x] Massachusetts
- [x] Michigan
- [x] Minnesota
- [ ] Mississippi
- [x] Missouri
- [ ] Montana
- [x] Nebraska
- [ ] Nevada
- [x] New Hampshire
- [x] New Jersey
- [x] New Mexico
- [x] New York
- [x] North Carolina

- [x] North Dakota
- [x] Ohio
- [x] Oklahoma
- [ ] Oregon
- [x] Pennsylvania
- [x] Rhode Island
- [x] South Carolina
- [x] South Dakota
- [x] Tennessee
- [x] Texas
- [ ] Utah
- [x] Vermont
- [x] Virginia
- [ ] Washington
- [x] West Virginia
- [x] Wisconsin
- [ ] Wyoming

CANADA [x]

THE TRAVEL BUG
© 1993 — The Learning Works, Inc.

License Plate Search No. 2

As you travel, look at vehicle license plates. Notice which state each plate is from. Place a mark in the large box beside a state name each time you see a plate from that state. When you reach your destination, count the marks and write the total in the small box beside each state name.

State	Number		State	Number		State	Number	
Ala.			La.			N. Dak.		
Alaska			Maine			Ohio		
Ariz.			Md.			Okla.		
Ark.			Mass.			Oreg.		
Calif.			Mich.			Pa.		
Colo.			Minn.			R.I.		
Conn.			Miss.			S.C.		
Del.			Mo.			S. Dak.		
Fla.			Mont.			Tenn.		
Ga.			Nebr.			Texas		
Hawaii			Nev.			Utah		
Idaho			N.H.			Vt.		
Ill.			N.J.			Va.		
Ind.			N. Mex.			Wash.		
Iowa			N.Y.			W. Va.		
Kans.			N.C.			Wis.		
Ky.						Wyo.		

State Plate Seen
Most Often _____

State Plate Seen
Least Often _____

Total Number of
Plates Counted _____

Tick-Tack-Toe Code

Tick-tack-toe code is an old code. It was used by the Confederate Army during the Civil War and has many variations. It is based on the positions of letters within a matrix and within the spaces formed by an X. In this code, each letter is represented by the lines which define the space that letter occupies. For example, ⌐ is A, ⊔ is B, and ∟ is C. Tick-tack-toe code is also called **pigpen code** because of the "fences" between the letters.

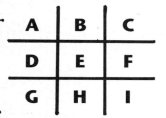  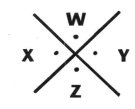

Use your knowledge of tick-tack-toe code to decode the answer to this question:

Where can a traveler always find money?

Answer:

In the space below, write a secret message in tick-tack-toe code.

84

THE TRAVEL BUG
© 1993 — The Learning Works, Inc.

Crack the Code

A code in which each letter of the alphabet is represented by a random symbol is called a **symbolic code**. As you might imagine, this randomness makes messages written in symbolic codes difficult to decipher—unless you know the code.

SYMBOLIC CODE

A	B	C	D	E	F	G	H	I	J	K	L	M
⛺	→	♀	÷	⛰	✳	🐦	☺	✺	⅁	♣	🐱	👤

N	O	P	Q	R	S	T	U	V	W	X	Y	Z
🍃	✤	⊗	🔒	⛢	♡	☆	⊙	♒	🐟	🍎	☺	👑

Decode the message written below to learn the answer to this riddle:

Which is the tallest building in every city you visit?

THE LIBRARY ALWAYS

HAS THE MOST STORIES

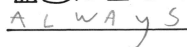

East-West Cryptogram

The English word **cryptogram** comes from two Greek words: *kryptos*, meaning "hidden or covered," and *gramma*, meaning "letter" and, by extension, "drawing, writing, or message." Thus, a cryptogram is a message or a communication that has been "hidden" in code.

There are two parts to this cryptogram, a question and its answer. Both have been encoded. Your challenge is to decode them.

The letters you see stand for other letters. Notice that the name of a city, **SAN FRANCISCO**, has been filled in. Look at the **S** in **SAN**. It is under the letter **W**; therefore, in this particular letter code, **W** stands for **S**. In the code box, write an **S** under the letter **W**. Then look for other **W**'s in the question and the answer. Write an **S** under any **W** that you find.

Follow these same steps for every letter in **SAN FRANCISCO**. Then see if you can fill in the other missing letters and decipher the cryptogram.

Question

Y B N E   Q U P W   N C C   E B P   Y N Z   H K U T

‾ ‾ ‾ ‾   ‾ ‾ ‾ ‾   ‾ ‾ ‾   ‾ ‾ ‾   ‾ ‾ ‾   ‾ ‾ ‾ ‾

J P Y   Z U K S   E U   W N J   H K N J O R W O U
‾ ‾ ‾   ‾ ‾ ‾ ‾   ‾ ‾   S̲A̲N̲   F̲R̲A̲N̲C̲I̲S̲C̲O̲

Y R E B U X E   T U L R J Q ?

‾ ‾ ‾ ‾ ‾ ‾ ‾   ‾ ‾ ‾ ‾ ‾ ‾

Answer

K N R C K U N A   E K N O S W

‾ ‾ ‾ ‾ ‾ ‾ ‾ ‾   ‾ ‾ ‾ ‾ ‾ ‾

Code Box									
A	B	C	D	E	F	G	H	I	J
K	L	M	N	O	P	Q	R	S	T
		U	V	W	X	Y	Z		

THE TRAVEL BUG
© 1993 — The Learning Works, Inc.

Bug Hunt

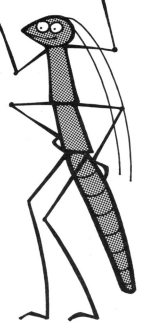

The names of thirty-one different bugs are hidden amid the letters below. See how many of them you can find. As you hunt, look horizontally (both from left to right and from right to left), vertically (both from top to bottom and from bottom to top), and diagonally.

```
A M I D G E F R E P P O H E E R T
D N A T U M B L E B U G U B E E T
I G T H B A E I E P A W A S P G R
D N T O K N D A L A P C U G U L E
Y I E R N T B T N A K O U B L O T
T W K N I I U G G S L B H A M W A
A E C E T S G N W N L S D G L W E
K C I T S G N I K L A W I W O O G
E A R W I G M R I U S T H O C R I
T L C L A M S P Q T N A P R U M F
I L I V E E W S Y L F Y A M S P Y
M O G R A S S H O P P E R A T N A
```

ANT	FLEA	LOCUST	SQUASHBUG
APHID	FROGHOPPER	LOUSE	STINKBUG
BACKSWIMMER	GNAT	MANTIS	TREEHOPPER
BAGWORM	GLOWWORM	MAYFLY	TUMBLEBUG
BEDBUG	GRASSHOPPER	MIDGE	WALKINGSTICK
BEE	HORNET	MITE	WASP
CRICKET	KATYDID	PILLBUG	WEEVIL
EARWIG	LACEWING	SPRINGTAIL	

THE TRAVEL BUG
© 1993 — The Learning Works, Inc.

Taxi! Taxi!

Aretha Arachnid is in a spin! She has tickets to hear the Grasshoppers in concert, and she wants to reach the theater before the music begins. She hails a taxicab and gives the somewhat befuddled driver these directions. Trace Aretha's route along the streets shown on page 89. If you follow her directions carefully, you may not reach the theater, but you will learn the name of the cab company Aretha called.

1. Start at the intersection of Ant Avenue and June Bug, and go east to Mayfly.
2. Go north on Mayfly until you reach Earwig. Turn left onto Earwig.
3. Go west on Earwig to June Bug, turn right, and go to Horse Fly.
4. Turn right again onto Horse Fly and go east to Queen Bee.
5. Make a U-turn and go back west on Horse Fly to Orthoptera.
6. Go south on Orthoptera to Ant Avenue, then turn onto Viceroy going northeast.
7. Take Viceroy all the way to Horse Fly, then turn and go south on Stonefly.
8. When you get to Dragonfly, turn and go two blocks west.
9. Make a U-turn when you reach Queen Bee, and go back to Stonefly.
10. Go south on Stonefly to Ant Avenue, then turn and go one block east to Termite.
11. Go north on Termite to Horse Fly.
12. At Horse Fly, turn right and go three blocks east to Water Strider.
13. Go south on Water Strider to Earwig, then take Earwig west to Gnat.
14. Turn left onto Gnat and go southeast to Ant Avenue.

THE TRAVEL BUG
© 1993 — The Learning Works, Inc.

Bugville Street Map

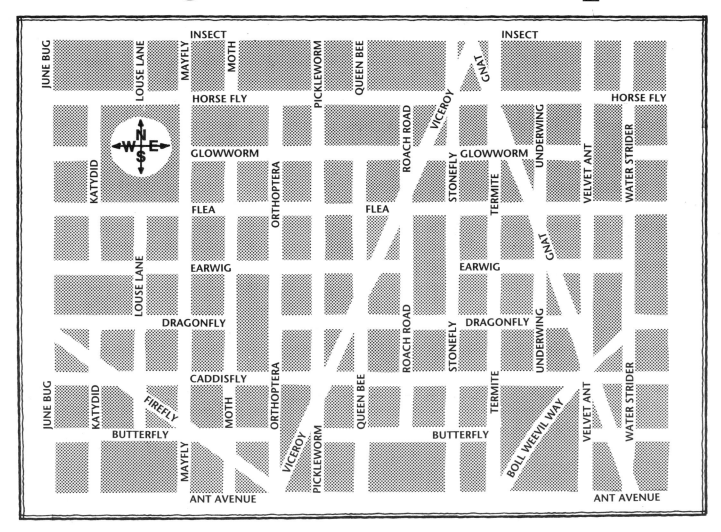

What is the name of the taxicab company? _____

Pozo, Ubly, and Yaak

Pozo, Ubly, Yaak, and the other words set in **bolder type** are the names of towns in the United States. On this page and on page 91 are some directions, and on page 91 are some boxed letters. Follow the directions carefully to connect the boxed letters and create a picture of something that could carry you from one of these towns to another. Take the steps in order, and check off each one as you complete it.

Draw a straight line from
- [ ] the fourth letter in **Bone** to the first letter in **Wynot**.
- [ ] the first letter in **Wynot** to the third letter in **Polo**.
- [ ] the third letter in **Polo** to the second letter in **Lulu**.
- [ ] the first letter in **Queets** to the third letter in **Nada**.
- [ ] the third letter in **Nada** to the fifth letter in **Moosic**.
- [ ] the first letter in **Yeso** to the first letter in **Salt**.
- [ ] the second letter in **Ajo** to the fourth letter in **Krum**.
- [ ] the second letter in **Ajo** to the third letter in **Loco**.
- [ ] the first letter in **Yeso** to the fourth letter in **Wing**.
- [ ] the first letter in **Vya** to the third letter in **Papa**.
- [ ] the fourth letter in **Yaak** to the third letter in **Tofty**.
- [ ] the second letter in **Lulu** to the second letter in **Thumb**.
- [ ] the first letter in **Rea** to the first letter in **Opp**.
- [ ] the fourth letter in **Wirt** to the fifth letter in **Moosic**.
- [ ] the third letter in **Fox** to the first letter in **Noti**.
- [ ] the first letter in **Noti** to the fourth letter in **Bone**.
- [ ] the second letter in **Mayo** to the first letter in **Queets**.
- [ ] the second letter in **Ubly** to the fourth letter in **Krum**.
- [ ] the second letter in **Ubly** to the second letter in **Mayo**.
- [ ] the second letter in **Thumb** to the first letter in **Opp**.
- [ ] the fourth letter in **Wing** to the first letter in **Rea**.
- [ ] the third letter in **Pozo** to the first letter in **Vya**.

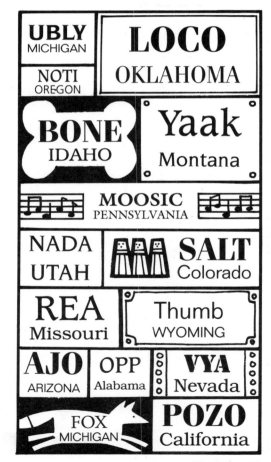

THE TRAVEL BUG
© 1993 — The Learning Works, Inc.

Pozo, Ubly, and Yaak
(continued)

QUEETS WASHINGTON

MAYO MARYLAND

WYNOT NEBRASKA

TOFTY Alaska

LULU FLORIDA

Draw a straight line from
- [ ] the third letter in **Papa** to the fourth letter in **Wirt**.
- [ ] the third letter in **Loco** to the third letter in **Tofty**.
- [ ] the third letter in **Pozo** to the first letter in **Salt**.
- [ ] the fourth letter in **Yaak** to the third letter in **Fox**.

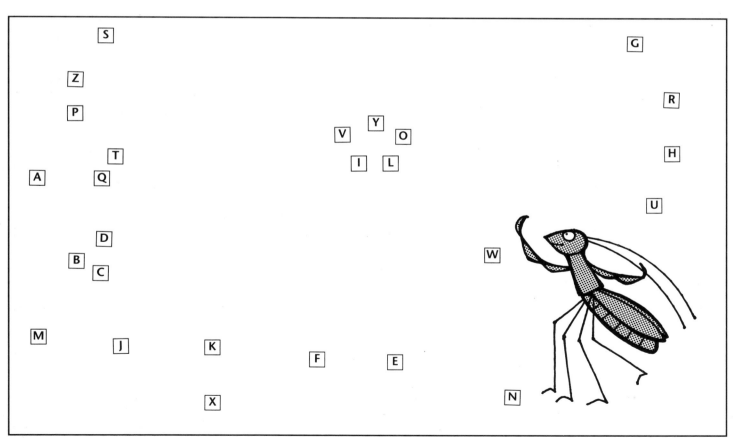

Answer Key

Page 54, Shade a Shape

The shaded shape is a one-humped camel, or dromedary. A creature of unusual speed, the dromedary is bred and trained especially for riding and is sometimes called the "ship of the desert."

Page 64, AUTOMOBILE Puzzle

Some of the words of three letters or more that can be made from the letters in the word AUTOMOBILE are

able	bloat	label	meat
aim	blue	lamb	melt
ale	boat	late	met
amble	boil	lie	mile
ate	bolt	lit	mit
atom	boom	loam	mite
bail	boot	lob	mob
bait	built	loom	moot
bat	bum	loot	mute
beat	but	lube	oat
belt	eat	lute	oboe
bile	emit	malt	table
bit	emu	mat	tame
blame	lab	mate	tube

Page 65, LOCOMOTIVE Puzzle

Some of the words of three letters or more that can be made from the letters in the word LOCOMOTIVE are

clot	lit	mole	toe
colt	live	moot	toil
cool	loom	motel	vet
coot	lot	motive	vice
cot	love	move	vie
ice	met	oil	vile
let	mice	tile	violet
lice	mile	time	voice

Page 66, HELICOPTER Puzzle

Some of the words of three letters or more that can be made from the letters in the word HELICOPTER are

cheer	heel	lop	reel
chip	help	lope	rice
choir	her	lore	rip
chop	here	lot	ripe
chore	hilt	ore	rite
cite	hip	peel	roe
clip	hire	pelt	role
coil	hit	pert	rope
cop	hoe	pet	rot
cope	hole	pierce	rote
core	hop	pile	the
corp	hope	pilot	their
cot	hot	pit	there
creep	hotel	plier	tile
crept	ice	plot	tiler
crop	ire	pole	tip
eel	let	police	tire
elect	lice	pore	top
elope	lip	pot	tore
	lit		trip

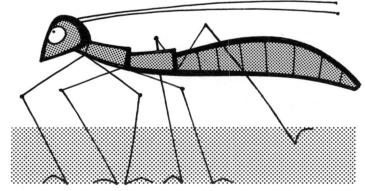

THE TRAVEL BUG
© 1993 — The Learning Works, Inc.

Answer Key
(continued)

Page 75, Suitcase Sums

6	16	2
4	8	12
14	0	10

1. The sum is 24.

9	19	5
7	11	15
17	3	13

2. The sum is 33.

10	20	6
8	12	16
18	4	14

3. The sum is 36.

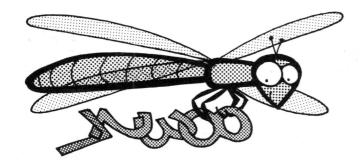

Page 76, Mystery in the Museum

Brett Butler left at 3:55.
Bessie Baker left at 4:05
Ben Babbitt left at 4:25.
Bobby Beaver left at 4:40.
Bruno Bailey left at 4:45.
Barbara Baez left at 4:55.
Bart Brown left at 5:10.
Betsy Bowers left at 5:15.
Betty Blair left at 5:20.
The special investigator took one look at these times of departure and concluded that Betty Blair was, indeed, the thief.

Page 78, Wonderful Word-a-Cycle

Some of the words of three letters or more which can be made using only the letters on the wheel (**D E I L M N T**) and following the rules of this game are

die	lid	linen	mint
dim	lie	lint	nil
dime	lien	lit	nine
din	lilt	men	nit
dine	lime	mid	tie
dint	limit	mild	tilt
emit	line	mine	time

Answer Key
(continued)

Page 79, Word Away
Some of the words of three letters or more which can be made using only the letters listed here (**A E K R S T W**) and following the rules of this game are

art	rake	seas	tar
arts	rakes	seat	tart
awake	rat	stake	tarts
awakes	rats	stakes	tsar
ear	raw	star	wake
ease	sake	start	wakes
eat	sat	starts	war
eats	saw	straw	wart
karat	sea	take	warts
karats	sear	takes	was

Page 80, Airport Dash

Page 81, Campward Bound

Page 84, Tick-Tack-Toe Code
In the dictionary

Page 85, Crack the Code
The library always has the most stories.

Page 86, East-West Cryptogram
Question: What goes all the way from New York to San Francisco without moving?
Answer: Railroad tracks

Page 87, Bug Hunt

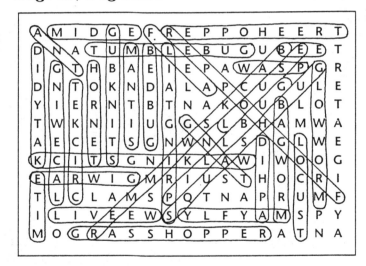

Page 88, Taxi! Taxi!
Aretha Arachnid rode in a taxi belonging to the Star Taxicab Company.

Pages 90–91, Pozo, Ubly, and Yaak
The thing that could carry you from Pozo to Ubly to Yaak and back is a helicopter.

THE TRAVEL BUG
© 1993 — The Learning Works, Inc.

JOURNAL PAGES
AND
KEEPSAKES

A Travel Journal

The English word **journal** comes from the Latin word *diurnus*, meaning "of a day, daily, the day's." Thus, a journal is a written record *of each day*.

The journal pages that follow provide a place for you to keep a written record of the things you do, the people you meet, the discoveries you make, and the feelings you have on each day of your trip.

At the end of the day, recall your thoughts and experiences. Then write about the things you want to remember. Include both challenges and accomplishments, the things that made you happy and the things that made you sad.

If you are short of ideas, consider the topics listed below. Write every day, even if your journal entries are brief. Then tuck this book away for safekeeping. You'll treasure the memories it contains in the years to come.

- the best part of your day
- the worst part of your day
- one thing you tried for the first time
- a place you visited
- a process you learned about or watched
- an interesting person you met
- a discovery you made
- something you learned about yourself
- something you would do differently next time
- a wish you would make for tomorrow

THE TRAVEL BUG
© 1993 — The Learning Works, Inc.

Date:_____ **Place:** _____

_____

_____

_____

_____

_____

_____

_____

_____

_____

Date:_____ **Place:** _____

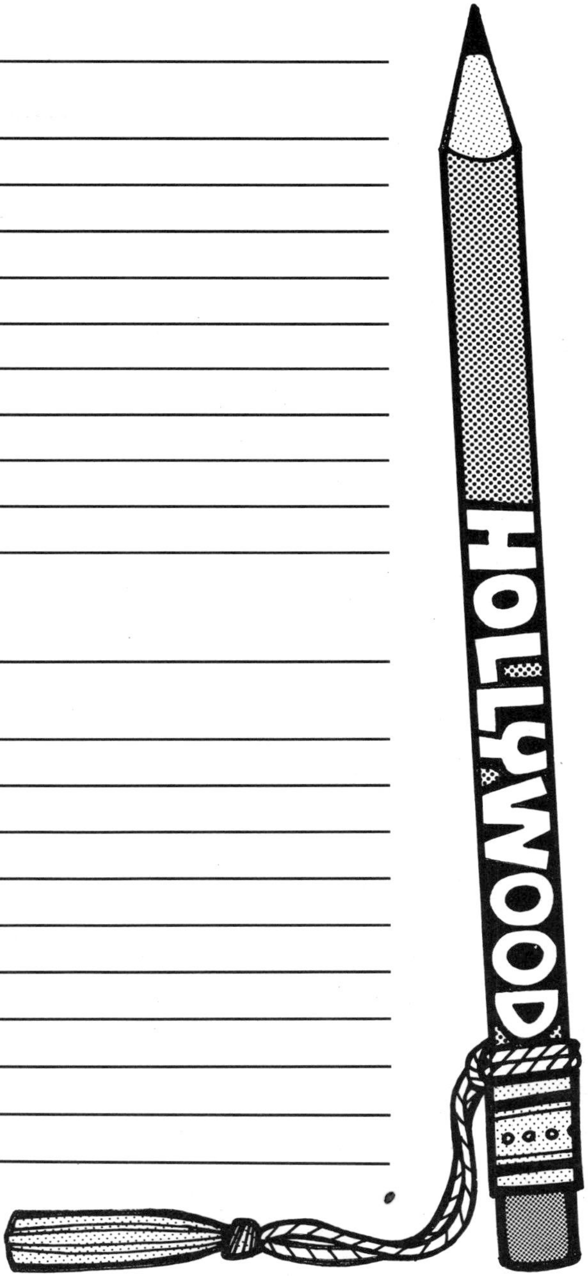

_____

_____

_____

_____

_____

_____

_____

_____

_____

CLOWN TOWN

Date:_____ **Place:**_____

_____

_____

_____

_____

_____

_____

_____

_____

_____

Date:_____ **Place:**_____

_____

_____

_____

_____

_____

_____

_____

_____

_____

_____

_____

THE TRAVEL BUG
© 1993 — The Learning Works, Inc.

Date:_____ **Place:** _____

_____

_____

_____

_____

_____

_____

_____

_____

Date:_____ **Place:** _____

_____

_____

_____

_____

_____

_____

_____

_____

_____

VALENTINE TEXAS

Date:_____ **Place:**_____

_____
_____
_____
_____
_____
_____
_____
_____
_____

Date:_____ **Place:**_____

_____
_____
_____
_____
_____
_____
_____
_____
_____

THE TRAVEL BUG
© 1993 — The Learning Works, Inc.

Date: _____ **Place:** _____

_____

_____

_____

_____

_____

_____

_____

_____

_____

Date: _____ **Place:** _____

_____

_____

_____

_____

_____

_____

_____

_____

_____

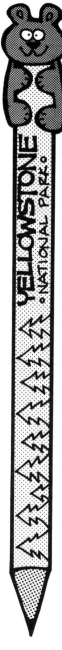

Date:_____ **Place:**_____

_____

_____

_____

_____

_____

_____

_____

_____

_____

Date:_____ **Place:**_____

_____

_____

_____

_____

_____

_____

_____

_____

_____

_____

THE TRAVEL BUG
© 1993 — The Learning Works, Inc.

Date: _____ **Place:** _____

_____

_____

_____

_____

_____

_____

_____

_____

_____

Date: _____ **Place:** _____

_____

_____

_____

_____

_____

_____

_____

_____

_____

BASEBALL MUSEUM

Date:_____   Place:_____

_____

_____

_____

_____

_____

_____

_____

_____

_____

_____

_____

Date:_____   Place:_____

_____

_____

_____

_____

_____

_____

_____

_____

_____

_____

_____

THE TRAVEL BUG
© 1993 — The Learning Works, Inc.

Date: _____ **Place:** _____

_____

_____

_____

_____

_____

_____

_____

_____

_____

Date: _____ **Place:** _____

_____

_____

_____

_____

_____

_____

_____

_____

_____

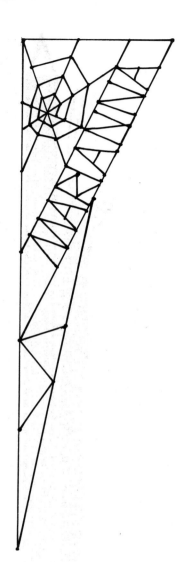

Autographs

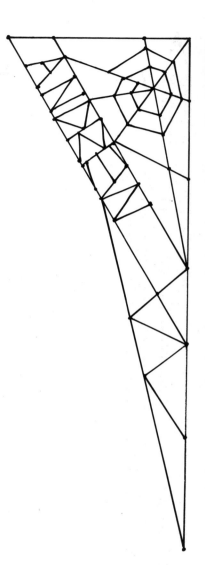

THE TRAVEL BUG
© 1993 — The Learning Works, Inc.

Autographs

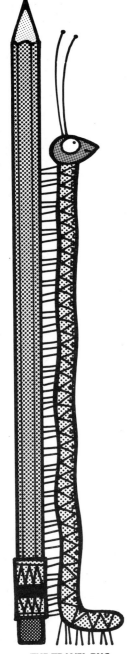

Autographs

THE TRAVEL BUG
© 1993 — The Learning Works, Inc.

Autographs

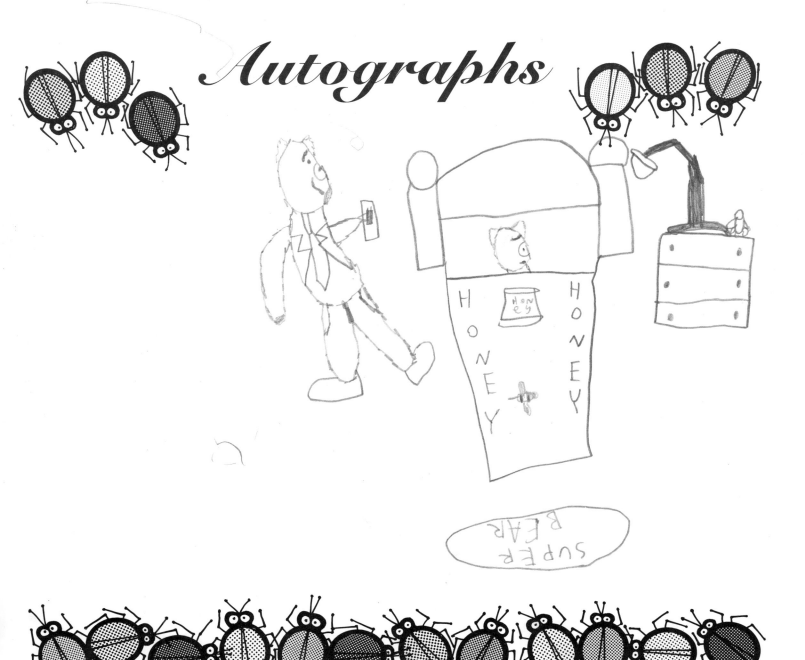

Snips & Snaps

Save those snips and snaps! Glue paper souvenirs from your trip — such as brochures, ticket stubs, pictures, postcards, empty sugar packets, napkins, and wrappers — on this page and the three that follow.

THE TRAVEL BUG
© 1993 — The Learning Works, Inc.

Snips & Snaps

Snips & Snaps

THE TRAVEL BUG
© 1993 — The Learning Works, Inc.

Snips & Snaps

Travel Sketchbook

In each box below, draw a picture of some special thing you saw during your travels and would like to remember.

THE TRAVEL BUG
© 1993 — The Learning Works, Inc.

Travel Sketchbook

In each box below, draw a picture of some special thing you saw during your travels and would like to remember.

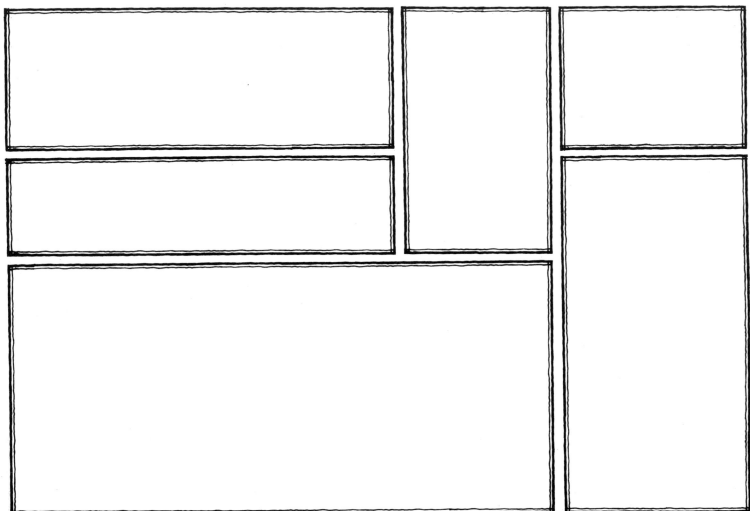

Travel Sketchbook

In each box below, draw a picture of some special thing you saw during your travels and would like to remember.

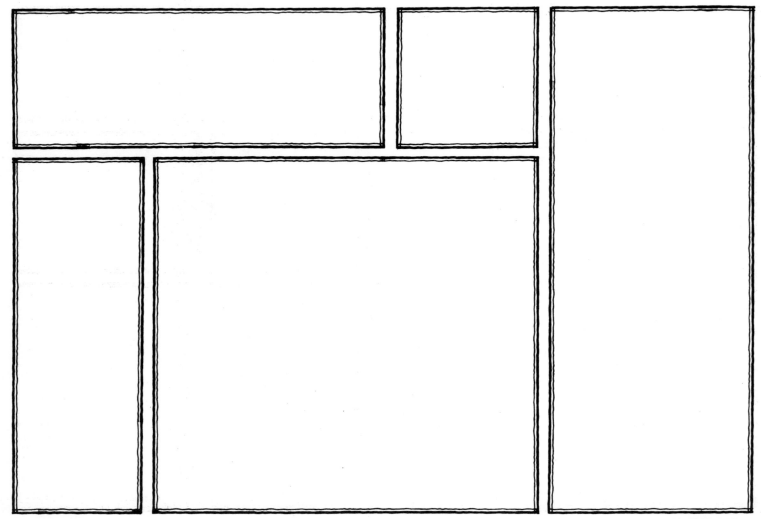

THE TRAVEL BUG
© 1993 — The Learning Works, Inc.

 # Travel Sketchbook

In each box below, draw a picture of some special thing you saw during your travels and would like to remember.

My Special Page

Use this page and the one that follows in any way you wish to keep a record of some of the special things you saw and did during your travels. For example, you might want to draw cartoons and add conversation, to attach photographs and write captions, or to create a montage of words and pictures from your trip.

THE TRAVEL BUG
© 1993 — The Learning Works, Inc.

My Special Page

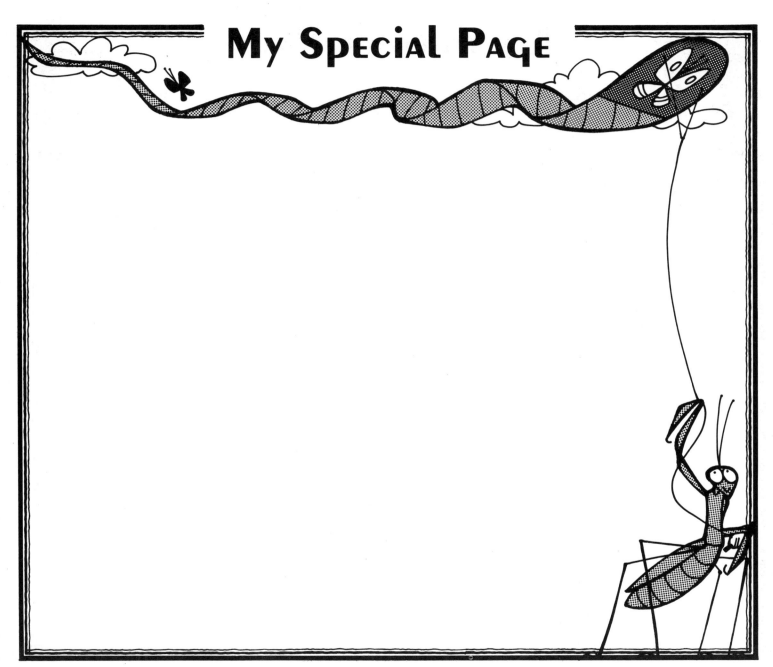

THE TRAVEL BUG
© 1993 — The Learning Works, Inc.

Keep in Touch

On the lines below, write the names and addresses of friends and relatives with whom you will want to keep in touch while you are away.

_____
(name)

_____
(number and street)

_____
(city, state, and zip code)

_____

_____

_____

_____

_____

_____

_____

_____
(name)

_____
(number and street)

_____
(city, state, and zip code)

_____

_____

_____

_____

_____

_____

_____

THE TRAVEL BUG
© 1993 — The Learning Works, Inc.